W9-BUI-523

Footprints on the Roof

poems about the earth

by **Marilyn Singer**

illustrated by **Meilo So**

Alfred A. Knopf
New York

For

Walter Mayes

and Valerie Lewis

THIS IS A BORZOI BOOK PUBLISHED BY ALFRED A. KNOPF

Text copyright © 2002 by Marilyn Singer
Illustrations copyright © 2002 by Meilo So

All rights reserved under International and Pan-American Copyright
Conventions. Published in the United States by Alfred A. Knopf, a division
of Random House, Inc., New York, and simultaneously in Canada by
Random House of Canada Limited, Toronto. Distributed by Random
House, Inc., New York. KNOPF, BORZOI BOOKS, and the colophon
are registered trademarks of Random House, Inc.

www.randomhouse.com/kids

Library of Congress Cataloging-in-Publication Data
Singer, Marilyn
Footprints on the roof : poems about the earth / by Marilyn Singer ;
illustrated by Meilo So.
p. cm.
ISBN 0-375-81094-3 (trade) — ISBN 0-375-91094-8 (lib. bdg.)
1. Earth—Juvenile poetry. 2. Children's poetry, American.
[1. Nature—Poetry. 2. Earth—Poetry. 3. American poetry.] I. So, Meilo, ill. II.
Title.
PS3569.I546 F66 2002
811'.54—dc21   2001029407

Manufactured in Malaysia

February 2002

10 9 8 7 6 5 4 3 2

First Edition

Contents

Home

Ask me where is home
            and I will tell you
                        a house
                        a street
                        a neighborhood
                        a town
Someplace safe and solid
            where I eat
                        I run
                            I sing
                            I nap
Someplace I can pinpoint
            on a map
But what if I were an astronaut
            with the world dangling below me
                        like a yo-yo from a giant's hand
            and home was the whole planet?
Would I be wise enough to understand
            the worth
                        of my new address: Earth

Burrows

Out in the country I walk across towns
       I'll never see:
mazy metropolises
      under the earth
           where rabbits hide from foxes
              foxes hide from dogs
              full-bellied snakes sleep snugly
                 worms work uncomplaining

Where what you see is nothing—
what counts is what you smell
         or hear or feel
I try to tread softly:
         a quiet giant
                  leaving only footprints
                           on the roof

7

Dining Out

Each day I eat the earth
       I drink the rain
They taste celery-bitter
          watermelon-sweet
Their flavor
      subtle
         bold
   is stored
in every grain of rice
     in every stalk of wheat
in every root
    leaf
    shoot
harvested in Chile
    or in China
       or at Fanelli's farm
Each day I eat the earth
    I drink the rain
And my tongue
          is never bored

9

Go-Betweens

Trees are go-betweens
       listening to the stories
of both earth and sky
        the conversations
of vireos and star-nosed moles
      of eagles and worms
Trees know the soft secrets of clouds
      the dark siftings of soil
They hear the high keening of squalls
        the deep rumbling of rocks
Trees whisper for the sky's damp blessings
     and the earth's misty kisses
They issue warnings
They offer praise
     This is trees' work
and they do it with such uncomplaining grace
      it never seems like work at all

II

Summer Solstice

Amid the scent of roses
  and the lulling hum of bees
comes a cloud scudding briefly across the sun
  or a slightly pointed breeze
to remind you that the earth has turned again
  and in a long slow wink
    the nights will grow
    the days will shrink
The richest garden
  the greenest trees
will have a different form
 wearing withered leaves like memories
   of days when it was warm

Natural Disasters

We were talking disasters
    scaring ourselves
        with what on earth would scare us:
Volcanoes venting red-hot rivers
        spumes of ash
    like barbecues gone crazy
Earthquakes that crack the world
    like a walnut
Sandstorms that suffocate
Tidal waves that drown
    Hurricanes, tornadoes
      avalanches, floods
And blizzards
    simple blizzards—
those frightened me the most
    trapping me right there in my house
      with nothing to eat
    but my shoes

We were talking disasters
     feeling the earth go wobbly
     leaving ourselves
       with no place to hide
Until right outside my window
     a robin chirruped loudly
       in the hickory tree
like nothing on earth mattered
     but its song
And suddenly the room righted itself
       the floor held steady
and we knew that we were safe
       for at least another day

Dormant Dragons

Volcanoes there are that sleep
    the sleep of dragons
With cool heads and hot bellies
    they crouch
        solid and still
    where the earth meets the sky
Till something wakes them
    Then furious they breathe fire and smoke
            hot spittle and wrath
      to burn and choke
        whatever lies in their path
    leaving in their wake
        an odd treasure
    of stone sponges and glass
        and an occasional lake

Caves

The thing about caves
      is you go so deep
           inside the earth
      you think that you have left it
Stalactites
      Stalagmites
Rivers made of crystal
      Flowers made of stone
Untraveled landscapes
      sunless
           moonless
from maybe some other galaxy
      where bats and beetles rule
and there are twenty words for darkness
      but none at all
                    for light

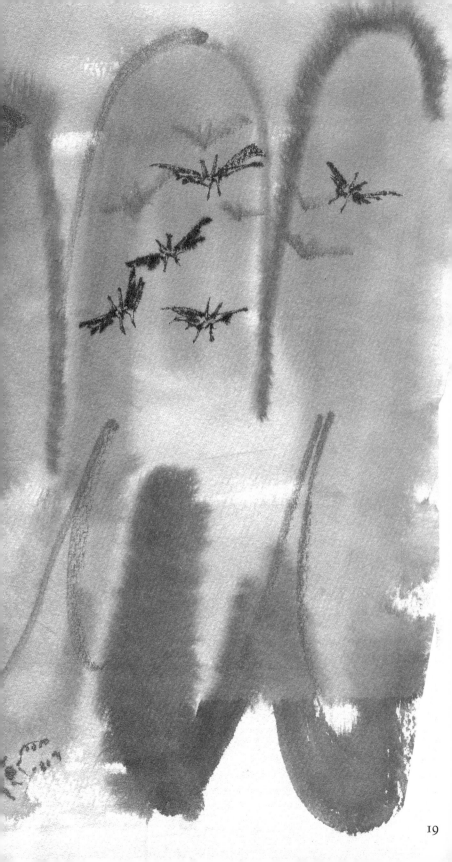

19

Prehistoric Praise

Dinosaurs get all the press
In books and movies
      on subway walls
           long-necked sauropods
           horn-headed triceratops
           sail-backs
                duck-bills
           and, yes indeed, terror-toothed Tyrannosaurus rex
                reign
Their big bones fill museum halls
Thrashing tail to gaping jaw
           they always inspire awe
But before
      way before reptiles ruled
      other creatures were here:
           sea scorpions the size of automobiles
           dragonflies the size of kites
           fish that climbed to shore
                on finny feet
           trilobites with twenty thousand eyes
           ancestral sharks and gliding rays
They left their shells
      their shape
      their ambition
    on the Earth
They too have worth
      They also amaze

Back to Nature

We cover the earth
  with asphalt
    tarmac
    concrete
    brick
We want to be far away
  from humus
    moss and leaf mold
  from things soft and unpredictable
    that slide beneath our feet
But even in the city
  sparrows nest in lampposts
    tree trunks rise from sewers
  and mulberries fat and purple
    rain on sidewalks
  turning the pavement soft and unpredictable
    making it slide beneath our feet

23

Mud

Sometimes I'm in the mood
                for mud
When my toes have tasted
        too many sidewalks
When my knees have stayed
        too clean
        too unused
When the earth is
        a cake without frosting
        or a sundae without sauce
Then I cheer on rain and thunder
        and forget about my shoes
In the park
        or by the river
I choose
                ooze

Winter Solstice

On December twenty-first
    shiny
        black-booted
    warmly snow-suited
I pick and lick an icicle
    and pretend I'm in Australia
where it is the first morning of summer
        on the other side of the earth
And I know that someone there
    sandy
        bare-footed
    coolly bathing-suited
will buy and try an ice cream cone
    and pretend she's in America
where it is the first morning of winter
        on the other side of the earth

Ice

The same night the window cracked
>the rain turned hard-hearted
>the ground turned mean
and we woke to a world of ice
Out on the street
>Dad windmilled like a slapstick dancer
>Mom crept like a mincing crab
We tried to tell them
>ice respects no one
If you can't lick it
>trick it
But they didn't want to hear
Then we looped our scarves across our faces
>so they couldn't see us laugh
and slid across the sidewalk
>like the earth was one big rink

Islands

Dad likes to talk
      about islands—
how they sink
how they rise
How some are bred
      by volcanoes
and others built from coral bones
How some are crowned by castles
and some stripped clean
      even of trees
It's the earth playing peek-a-boo
      with the sea, he says
But to me it sounds
      a more dangerous game
And I think once in a while the sea
      just finds it amusing
         to let the earth
           win

Fens

I'm a fan of fens
  of bogs, marshes and bayous—
those in-between places of the earth
  not quite water, not quite land
those untrustworthy places
  that make you watch where you stand
those horror movie places
  damp and thick with fog
full of jaws and flashing claws,
    scales and thrashing tails
You can't be bored in a bayou
  a fen, a marsh, a bog—
those misunderstood places
    where logs can have teeth
    reeds can have wings
  where the air so still, so quiet
always growls, buzzes, sings

33

Desert

I want to be there when the desert blooms
To see hot pink and shining gold
      interrupt the endless tan
To dance among the cactuses
      sporting flowers in their spiky hair
To celebrate the birth of tadpoles
      swimming in sudden pools

I want to be there when the desert blooms
To watch this serious span of earth
      grow festive for a day
To revel in rain as something
      sacred and rare
To honor this peculiar place
      where hope is not for fools

Dunes

There are dunes
      and there are dunes
Standing on the earth
      flat-footed and thirsty
we see only relentless sand
But from up high
      we gaze with pleasure
          at ripples and ridges
            crescents and spheres—
every dune a signature
      announcing its creator
each one a sculpture
      in a worldwide work of art

Patience

I thought I would be taller
    in the mountains
A queen of green and brown
    my realm laid out below me
        neat as the rug Grandma hooked
    one St. Patrick's Day

I thought I would be braver
    in the mountains
Following the fierce paths
    of pumas and grizzlies
Ledge leaper
    Crag climber
Taking nothing for granted
    Leaving nothing unexplored

I thought I would be wiser
    in the mountains
Reading the history of the world
    in the weathered rocks
Hearing lectures
    in the wind and waterfalls
Stretching my mind
    broader than Grandpa's tall stories
        multiplied by ten

I thought I would be taller
                    braver
                    wiser
        in the mountains
And I wasn't
But I am more patient
        in the mountains
And I can wait

Early Explorers

No place on earth
      is ever undiscovered
Even in Antarctica
      where whole mountains are hidden
         under ice
penguins already laid shambling tracks
         in the snow
      before we traveled there
The hottest desert
         the deepest jungle
      where none of us have ever been
all have been crossed
         and crossed again
      by wings whirring or silent
         feet furred or scaled
            hoofed or bare
By adventurers we will never know
      explorers who will never tell us
         what wonders they have seen